SHEIKH ZAYED GRAND MOSQUE

Simon Rose

www.av2books.com

AV² provides enriched content that supplements and complements this book. Weigl's AV² books strive to create inspired learning and engage young minds in a total learning experience.

Your AV² Media Enhanced books come alive with...

Audio
Listen to sections of the book read aloud.

Key Words
Study vocabulary, and complete a matching word activity.

Video
Watch informative video clips.

Quizzes
Test your knowledge.

Go to www.av2books.com, and enter this book's unique code.

Embedded Weblinks
Gain additional information for research.

Slide Show
View images and captions, and prepare a presentation.

BOOK CODE

H482239

AV² by Weigl brings you media enhanced books that support active learning.

Try This!
Complete activities and hands-on experiments.

... and much, much more!

Published by AV² by Weigl
350 5th Avenue, 59th Floor
New York, NY 10118
Websites: www.av2books.com   www.weigl.com

Library of Congress Cataloging-in-Publication Data
Rose, Simon, 1961-
 Sheikh Zayed Al Nahyan Grand Mosque / Simon Rose.
    pages cm. -- (Houses of faith)
 Includes bibliographical references and index.
 ISBN 978-1-4896-2612-7 (hardcover : alk. paper) -- ISBN 978-1-4896-2616-5 (softcover : alk. paper) -- ISBN 978-1-4896-2620-2 (single-user ebk.) -- ISBN 978-1-4896-2624-0 (multi-user ebk.)
 1. Jami' al-Shaykh Zayid al-Kabir (Abu Zaby, United Arab Emirates)--Juvenile literature. 2. Mosques--United Arab Emirates--Abu Zaby--Juvenile literature.
 3. Abu Zaby (United Arab Emirates)--Buildings, structures, etc.--Juvenile literature. I. Title.
 NA5973.2.A28J367 2014
 726'.2095357--dc23
                          2014038574

Printed in the United States of America in North Mankato, Minnesota
1 2 3 4 5 6 7 8 9 0 18 17 16 15 14

112014
WEP311214

Editor: Heather Kissock
Design: Mandy Christiansen

Every reasonable effort has been made to trace ownership and to obtain permission to reprint copyright material. The publishers would be pleased to have any errors or omissions brought to their attention so that they may be corrected in subsequent printings. Weigl acknowledges Getty Images, Alamy, Corbis, iStockphoto, and Dreamstime as its primary image suppliers for this title.

Contents

What Is the Sheikh Zayed Grand Mosque?

The Sheikh Zayed Grand Mosque is the most important place of worship for Muslims in the United Arab Emirates (UAE). Located in Abu Dhabi, it is the largest mosque in the country and the eighth largest mosque in the world. Besides being a key place of worship, the mosque is also a popular tourist attraction. Its soaring towers, onion-shaped domes, and pure white coloring attract visitors from around the world.

The mosque was constructed between 1996 and 2007. The driving force behind the building of the mosque was Sheikh Zayed bin Sultan Al Nahyan, the first president of the UAE. Sheikh Zayed wanted the mosque to reflect the many different cultures that make up the **Islamic** world. Many types of art and **architecture** influenced the mosque's design.

Sheikh Zayed did not live to see the mosque completed. When he died in 2004, his funeral became the first ceremony to be held in the mosque. Today, his **mausoleum** sits to the north of the mosque.

The Sheikh Zayed Grand Mosque is considered by many to be one of the best examples of modern Islamic architecture.

The Islamic Faith

Muslims believe that Islam has always existed, but was revealed to people over time by a series of **prophets**. The prophet Muhammad revealed the final elements of the religion in the 7th century AD. In Arabic, the word *islam* means "surrender." The religion is based on the idea of surrendering to the will of God. Muslims believe that there is only one God. The Arabic word for God is *Allah*. To discover the will of Allah, Muslims read a holy book called the Qur'an. This book sets the rules for how Muslims are to live their lives.

There are five basic Pillars of Islam. These are declaring faith, praying five times a day, giving money to charity, fasting, and making a **pilgrimage** to the city of Mecca, in Saudi Arabia, at least once in a lifetime.

Islam is the
2nd largest
religion in the world. There are about 1.6 billion Muslims worldwide.

There are two main groups of Muslims.
About 90%
of Muslims are Sunnis. Most other Muslims are Shia.

Indonesia has the world's
LARGEST
Muslim population, at more than 200 million.

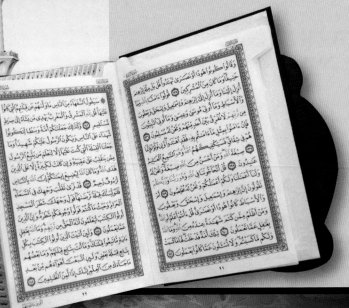

The Qur'an has
114 chapters.

A Step Back in Time

Sheikh Zayed bin Sultan Al Nahyan wanted to create a mosque that symbolized the different beliefs of Islam. However, he also believed that the mosque should promote **tolerance** and peace among people of various religious and cultural backgrounds. He wanted the mosque to be a place that brought people together.

The construction project was seen as one way to unite different cultures. The mosque's design was inspired by architecture from the Middle East, North Africa, Pakistan, and India. Companies from around the world contributed to the building's construction. The materials used to build the mosque also came from many different countries.

CONSTRUCTION TIMELINE

2003 The basic framework for the mosque, including its **foundation**, is completed. Work begins on the interior.

Late 1980s Plans are first made to build the mosque. Architectural designs are completed and approved over the next few years.

1996 Construction of the mosque officially begins on November 5.

1990 | **2000** | **2001** | **2002** | **2003**

2001 British construction company Halcrow becomes the project's **consulting engineers** in October.

2002 The concrete shell of the mosque is completed in May.

Sheikh Zayed added many of his own ideas to the project. Not only did he select the mosque's location, he also made suggestions about its **dimensions** and the materials and colors that should be used. When the mosque was completed in 2007, it was the culmination of Sheikh Zayed's initial dream and vision.

Sheikh Zayed was one of the founders of the United Arab Emirates. He is often referred to as the "Father of the Nation" because of his work in bringing the emirates together.

2004
Sheikh Zayed bin Sultan Al Nahyan dies. His son, Sheikh Khalifa bin Zayed Al Nahyan, continues his father's work on the mosque.

2007 On December 20, the mosque officially opens to the public.

| 2004 | 2006 | 2008 | 2009 | 2010 |

2006 Under the supervision of Dr. Ali Khaliqi, more than 1,200 workers begin making the world's largest hand-woven carpet. It is completed 21 months later and placed in the mosque's main prayer hall.

2008 The Sheikh Zayed Grand Mosque Center is founded to provide information about the mosque and its founder.

2010 The Sheikh Zayed Grand Mosque library opens in the mosque's north **minaret**.

The Mosque's Location

The Sheikh Zayed Grand Mosque sits in the newer part of Abu Dhabi, the capital city of the UAE. The mosque is located between the Musaffah Bridge, the Maqta Bridge, and the Sheikh Zayed Bridge, all of which link the city to the mainland.

DOME The main dome is 278.9 feet (85 meters) in height from the outside, with a **diameter** of 107.6 feet (32.8 m). Its inside height reaches 229.7 feet (70 m).

COURTYARD The courtyard covers an area of about 183,000 square feet (17,000 square meters).

The Sheikh Zayed Grand Mosque holds a prominent location in the city and is one of the first buildings people see as they enter Abu Dhabi from the mainland.

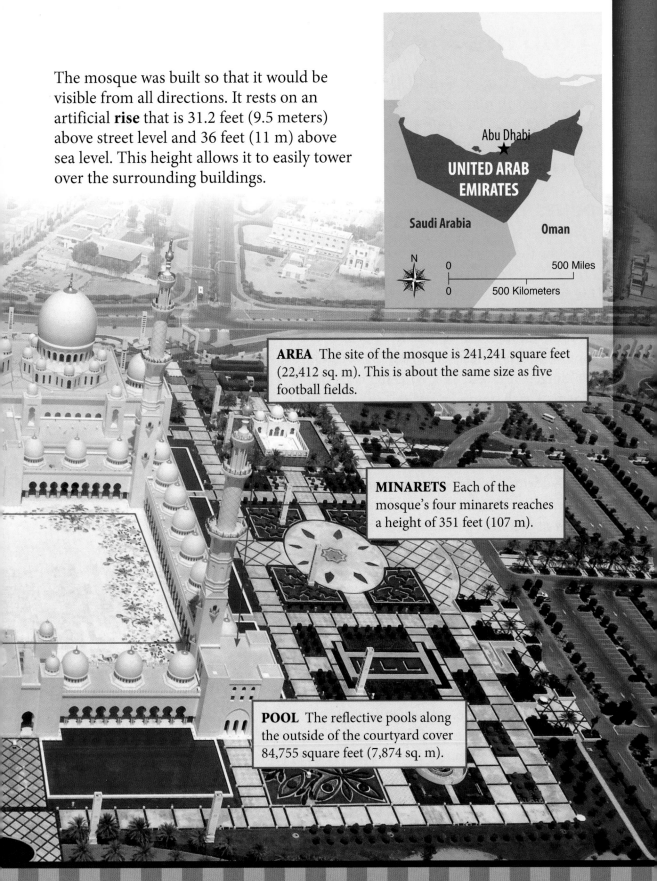

The mosque was built so that it would be visible from all directions. It rests on an artificial **rise** that is 31.2 feet (9.5 meters) above street level and 36 feet (11 m) above sea level. This height allows it to easily tower over the surrounding buildings.

Abu Dhabi

UNITED ARAB EMIRATES

Saudi Arabia

Oman

N

0   500 Miles

0   500 Kilometers

AREA The site of the mosque is 241,241 square feet (22,412 sq. m). This is about the same size as five football fields.

MINARETS Each of the mosque's four minarets reaches a height of 351 feet (107 m).

POOL The reflective pools along the outside of the courtyard cover 84,755 square feet (7,874 sq. m).

Touring the Exterior

The Sheikh Zayed Grand Mosque features many design elements common to Muslim architecture. These elements have been arranged in such a way as to reflect the peace and tranquility of the Islam faith.

DOMES The mosque's many domes are one of its most striking features. Made of marble, they line the outer walls of the mosque, sit atop entrances, and form its central core. The biggest dome covers the mosque's main prayer hall. It is the largest mosque dome in the world. At the bottom of each dome are a series of long windows. These let natural light into the building. A crescent-shaped **finial** caps the crown of each dome.

COURTYARD The mosque's large outdoor courtyard is known as the Sahan. The courtyard is paved with white and colored marble. Its outer border is lined with elaborate floral designs. A row of columns surrounds the courtyard. The pools around the outer courtyard reflect the white and gold columns during the day. At night, the scene is transformed. A special lighting system is used to reflect the phases of the Moon.

MINARETS Each corner of the courtyard features a tall minaret. The towers have one or more balconies. In the past, a **muezzin** called worshippers to prayer while standing on a balcony near the top of a minaret. Today, microphones and electronic speakers are used to call people for prayer at the mosque. The minarets themselves are used to house office space and other rooms.

The reflective pools running along the sides of the courtyard are shallow and for decoration only.

The mosque's minarets are lit at night and serve as beacons for aircraft.

A series of arcades, or walkways, surrounds the mosque's courtyard.

Large glass doors lead into the main prayer hall.

A prayer clock hangs by the mosque's main entrance. The clock shows the five prayer times for the day.

Like the domes, the minarets also feature a crescent-shaped finial.

$ $ $ $ $ $

It cost **$545 million USD** to build the Sheikh Zayed Grand Mosque.

More than 1,000 columns line the outside of the Sahan.

The mosque's outer columns are covered with more than **20,000** marble panels. These are decorated with semi-precious stones.

The mosque's main glass door is **40 feet** (12.2 m) high and **22.9 feet** (7 m) wide. It weighs about **2.4 tons** (2.2 tonnes).

The mosque features 28 types of marble from all over the world.

The Sheikh Zayed Grand Mosque has 82 domes.

Touring the Interior

The mosque was created as a place of worship. Many of its rooms were created specifically for this purpose. Others serve as areas for people to prepare for worship or to learn about Islam.

PRAYER HALLS The Sheikh Zayed Grand Mosque has three main prayer halls. The largest prayer hall can hold more than 7,000 people, while the open prayer hall holds about 2,000. Women have a separate prayer hall. It can fit about 1,000 worshippers. The main prayer hall is easily recognized by its size and decoration. The room features 96 marble columns, situated to support the weight of the main dome. From the center of the dome hangs a massive chandelier decorated with thousands of sparkling crystals.

ABLUTION ROOMS Muslims believe that they must enter a state of purity before they begin to pray. This purity is achieved through cleanliness. Before entering the prayer hall, worshippers visit one of the mosque's **ablution** rooms, which are located in the basement of the building. The mosque has two ablution rooms. One is for men, and the other is for women. The center of each room features a large fountain, where people can wash themselves and prepare to pray.

LIBRARY Located on the third floor of the north minaret, the mosque's library was developed to show the scope of Islamic culture. The library contains books about science, the arts, coins, and civilization. It houses more than 50,000 rare editions of **manuscripts** and prints, and features copies of the Qur'an that date back to the 1500s.

The 99 names of Allah are written on the mosque's Qibla wall. This wall faces toward Mecca. Muslims face the wall when praying.

Marble seating surrounds the fountains in the ablution rooms.

The chandelier in the main prayer hall is 49 feet (15 m) tall and measures 33 feet (10 m) in diameter.

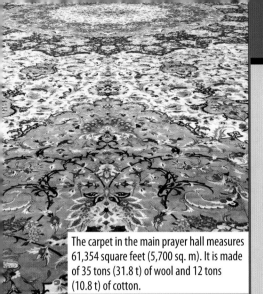

The carpet in the main prayer hall measures 61,354 square feet (5,700 sq. m). It is made of 35 tons (31.8 t) of wool and 12 tons (10.8 t) of cotton.

At the request of Sheikh Zayed, many of the mosque's walls are decorated with elaborate floral patterns.

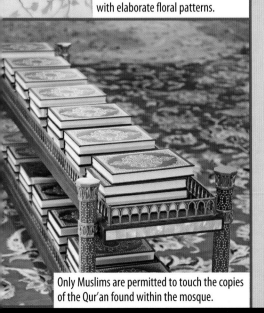

Only Muslims are permitted to touch the copies of the Qur'an found within the mosque.

The carpet in the main prayer hall is so large that it had to be shipped to the mosque on two separate flights.

The mosque has **7** chandeliers. Together, they are priced at more than **$8** million USD.

The chandelier in the main prayer hall weighs **13 tons** (12 t).

More than **3 million** people visit the Sheikh Zayed Grand Mosque every year.

The mosque is **CLOSED** to tourists on Friday mornings. Only worshippers can enter at this time.

The mosque can hold **40,960** worshippers at one time.

Admission to the mosque is free.

The Science behind the Mosque

The building of the Sheikh Zayed Grand Mosque was a massive engineering and construction project. Great care was taken during the design phase and at each stage of development. The mosque's dimensions, durability, and safety all had to be considered. The designers also had to ensure that the mosque would be suitable and comfortable for worshippers and visitors.

CONCRETE AND STEEL The Sheikh Zayed Grand Mosque has a reinforced concrete shell. Concrete is known for its strength and its ability to stand up to many of the conditions a building will experience. To make it even stronger, builders often reinforce the concrete. When reinforcing concrete, metal bars are placed inside a mold, and concrete is added. Once the concrete sets, the bars bond to it. This strengthens the concrete and allows it to withstand the natural forces that act upon it. About 36,376 tons (33,000 t) of steel reinforcement were used during the mosque's construction. Approximately 7,416,080 cubic feet (210,000 cubic meters) of concrete were also used. The steel and concrete sit on 6,500 foundation **piles**.

DOMES Domes are considered one of the strongest structures that can be built. A dome curves both horizontally and vertically. This double curve evenly distributes the weight of the dome throughout the structure underneath. The weight of the top spreads down in such a way that no area receives more pressure than any other. Strong foundations are needed to support the weight of the mosque's main dome over such a wide space. The **ring beam** supporting the main dome is 16.4 feet (5 m) deep.

ARCHES **Arches** can be found throughout the mosque. They curve over hallways, entrances, and **colonnades**. Arches have been used in construction for centuries. They can span great distances and carry heavy weight. **Gravity** causes the weight of a structure to press downward. With an arch, this pressure is changed from a downward force to an outward force. The outward force spreads the weight of the structure evenly across a larger area. The arches used in the Sheikh Zayed Grand Mosque are both decorative and functional. They help to beautify the building while also helping to support the weight of the building's roof and domes.

The use of arches in the arcades is typical of Islamic architecture.

The dome evolved from the arch. In fact, a dome can be thought of as an arch rotated 360 degrees on its axis.

The arches surrounding the main prayer hall are pointed. A pointed arch is able to support up to three times more weight than a rounded arch.

Placing steel bars in the concrete allows a structure to better resist forces such as wind and vibration.

The Mosque's Builders

Many people were involved in bringing Sheikh Zayed's vision for the mosque to life. Family members played a key role in the project, while more than 3,000 workers and 38 contracting companies from all over the world took part in the mosque's construction.

Sheikh Zayed bin Sultan Al Nahyan

Sheikh Zayed bin Sultan Al Nahyan was born in 1918 as the youngest son of Sheikh Sultan bin Zayed al Nahyan, the ruler of the emirate of Abu Dhabi. Sheikh Zayed became the emirate's ruler himself in 1966. Almost five years later, he was chosen to be the first president of the UAE. He used the wealth created by the region's oil industry to improve the country. During his presidency, schools, housing developments, hospitals, and roads were built, and more people moved to the area. The mosque is symbolic of the changes Sheikh Zayed brought to the UAE. It represents the transformation of the UAE into a modern country.

Sheikh Khalifa bin Zayed Al Nahyan

Sheikh Khalifa bin Zayed Al Nahyan succeeded his father as president of the UAE and has continued the work of his father in modernizing the country. He also played a key role in ensuring the completion of the Sheikh Zayed Grand Mosque. Prior to becoming president, Sheikh Khalifa held several high-ranking government positions. Today, he is the chairman of the Abu Dhabi Investment Council (ADIC), which manages the wealth of the UAE. He also founded the Khalifa bin Zayed Al Nahyan Foundation, which focuses on health and education issues at the local and global level.

Even though family members completed the mosque, they made sure that the building remained true to Sheikh Zayed's vision.

Sheikh Mohammed bin Zayed Al Nahyan

Sheikh Mohammed bin Zayed Al Nahyan is the current **crown prince** of Abu Dhabi. He is also the Deputy Supreme Commander of the UAE Armed Forces. Sheikh Mohammed was involved in the completion of the Sheikh Zayed Grand Mosque following his father's death. Today, he plays a large role in the economic development of the UAE. He has worked hard to raise educational standards and improve healthcare in the country. Sheikh Mohammed is a strong supporter of green technologies and clean energy. He has donated billions of dollars to charity for various causes. In 2010, Sheikh Mohammed accompanied Queen Elizabeth II of the United Kingdom during her official visit to the Sheikh Zayed Grand Mosque.

Sheikh Mansour bin Zayed Al Nahyan

Sheikh Mansour bin Zayed Al Nahyan is the Deputy Prime Minister and Minister of Presidential Affairs of the UAE. He is the half brother of Sheikh Khalifa. In 2007, Sheikh Mansour became chairman of the Emirates Investment Authority. This organization invests money on behalf of the UAE government. He is also in charge of several other government organizations. Sheikh Mansour played a key role in the completion of the Grand Mosque project. In 2010, he officially opened the library at the Sheikh Zayed Grand Mosque Centre. Sheikh Mansour is also the owner of the Manchester City Football Club in the United Kingdom.

Similar Structures around the World

Mosques can be found in various parts of the world. Some of these mosques have been on Earth for more than 1,400 years. Others have been built more recently. Many of these mosques have design features similar to those found in the Sheikh Zayed Grand Mosque.

Badshahi Mosque

BUILT: 1674
LOCATION: Lahore, Pakistan
DESIGN: Emperor Aurangzeb, Muzaffar Hussain
DESCRIPTION: The Badshahi Mosque is the fifth largest mosque in the world and the second largest in Pakistan and South Asia. The Badshahi Mosque can accommodate 55,000 worshippers in the main prayer hall. The mosque features four minarets, a vast courtyard, a grand entrance gate, and several domes. The exterior is made mainly of red sandstone that has been decorated with carvings and marble **inlay**.

The design of the Badshahi Mosque was influenced by the architecture of other parts of the world, including Persia, India, and central Asia.

Al-Fateh Mosque

BUILT: 1988
LOCATION: Manama, Bahrain
DESIGN: Sheikh Issa bin Salman Al Khalifa
DESCRIPTION: The Al-Fateh Mosque is one of the largest mosques in the world. It covers an area of 69,965 square feet (6,500 sq. m) and can accommodate more than 7,000 worshippers. Two minarets rise above the structure. Each is about 230 feet (70 m) in height. The mosque's dome is made of **fiberglass**. It weighs more than 60 tons (54 t) and features 12 stained glass windows. Italian marble was used for the floors and parts of the mosque's walls. Many of the walls are decorated with **calligraphy**. Besides being a place of worship, the building also houses the national library of Bahrain.

The Al-Fateh Mosque was named after Ahmed Al Fateh, the man who conquered Bahrain in 1783.

More than 5,000 workers were hired to help with the construction of Jama Masjid.

Jama Masjid

BUILT: 1656
LOCATION: Delhi, India
DESIGN: Shah Jahan
DESCRIPTION: Located in the old part of Delhi, Jama Masjid is the largest and best-known mosque in India. The mosque has three gates and four towers. Its two minarets are 131 feet (40 m) high and are built from strips of white marble and red sandstone. The large courtyard is paved with red stone and can hold 25,000 worshippers at one time. Carvings and text from the Qur'an decorate the mosque's walls. The mosque also contains several ancient Islamic **relics**, including items that once belonged to the prophet Muhammad.

Issues Facing the Mosque

Large religious buildings such as the Sheikh Zayed Grand Mosque are expected to stand for hundreds of years. Care needs to be taken during construction to use long-lasting materials. Builders also need to consider the environment and weather in the area where the mosque is to be constructed.

WHAT IS THE ISSUE?

The UAE is in a part of the world that has earthquakes.	The UAE can experience extreme weather conditions.

EFFECTS

Earthquakes could cause damage to the mosque or put it in danger of collapse.	High temperatures, sandstorms, and humidity could cause the building to experience **weathering** over time.

ACTION TAKEN

The designers and builders of the mosque used strong materials and built solid foundations. This helps to prevent damage in the event of an earthquake.	The marble used in the mosque's construction was chosen for its ability to withstand the country's environmental conditions.

Test the Strength of an Arch

Arches are used to support heavy weights using minimal materials. They are cost-effective and strong. Arches are also architecturally attractive. Try this activity to see how arches really work.

Materials
- Six eggs
- Heavy books
- Cellophane tape
- Scissors

Instructions
1. Break off the smallest end of each egg. Pour the insides into a bowl. Store them in a fridge to cook or bake with later. Throw out the broken ends.

2. Take six long pieces of cellophane tape. Wind a piece around the center of each eggshell.

3. Cut through the center of the tape. You should now have six dome-shaped shells.

4. Lay the six domes on a table in a rectangle. Make sure the flat side is down.

5. Estimate how many books you can lay across the domes.

6. Now, lay the books one by one across the dome. See how many books you can lay down before the shells break.

Sheikh Zayed Grand Mosque Quiz

Q Where is the Sheikh Zayed Grand Mosque located?

A In the city of Abu Dhabi in the UAE

Q How many worshippers can the mosque hold?

A 40,960

Q How much did it cost to build the mosque?

A $545 million USD

Q How many domes are in the mosque?

A 82

Key Words

ablution: the act of washing oneself

arches: curved structures that span an opening

architecture: the design of buildings and other structures

calligraphy: the art of stylized handwriting

colonnades: a series of columns placed at regular intervals

consulting engineers: people who advise builders on the scientific and mathematical principles needed to construct buildings and other structures

crown prince: the male heir to a throne

diameter: the length of a line that passes through the center of a circle from one side to the other

dimensions: measurements in length, width, and depth

fiberglass: a reinforced plastic material made of glass fibers and resin

finial: an ornament at the top of an object

foundation: construction below the ground that distributes the load of a building or structure built on top of it

gravity: the force that pulls objects toward the center of Earth

inlay: a design, pattern, or piece of material placed in another material

Islamic: relating to the religion of Islam

manuscripts: books or other documents

mausoleum: a building that houses a burial chamber

minaret: a tall tower of a mosque

muezzin: a man who calls Muslims to prayer from the minaret of a mosque

piles: long, slender columns of wood or metal that are pounded into the ground to support the weight of a structure

pilgrimage: a journey to a religious place to show devotion

prophets: people who deliver messages believed to come from God

relics: ancient objects revered by religious followers

ring beam: a form of horizontal support used in construction

rise: an increase in height

tolerance: respecting the beliefs of others

weathering: changes brought to buildings and other structures by climate and environmental conditions

Index

Log on to www.av2books.com

AV² by Weigl brings you media enhanced books that support active learning. Go to www.av2books.com, and enter the special code found on page 2 of this book. You will gain access to enriched and enhanced content that supplements and complements this book. Content includes video, audio, weblinks, quizzes, a slide show, and activities.

AV² Online Navigation

Audio
Listen to sections of the book read aloud.

Book Pages
AV² pages directly correspond to pages in the book.

Video
Watch informative video clips.

Key Words
Study vocabulary, and complete a matching word activity.

Embedded Weblinks
Gain additional information for research.

Quizzes
Test your knowledge.

Slide Show
View images and captions, and prepare a presentation.

Try This!
Complete activities and hands-on experiments.

AV² was built to bridge the gap between print and digital. We encourage you to tell us what you like and what you want to see in the future.

Sign up to be an AV² Ambassador at www.av2books.com/ambassador.